100 AutoCAD Exercises

Learn by Practicing (2nd Edition)

Create CAD Drawings by Practicing with AutoCAD

CADArtifex

The premium provider of learning products and solutions
www.cadartifex.com

100 AutoCAD Exercises - Learn by Practicing (2nd Edition)

Published by
CADArtifex
www.cadartifex.com

NOTICE TO THE READER

The publisher and the author make no representations or warranties with respect to the accuracy or completeness of the contents of this work/text and specifically disclaim all warranties, including without limitation warranties of fitness for a particular purpose. Publisher does not guarantee any of the products described in the text or perform any independent analysis in connection with any of the product information contained in the text. No warranty may be created or extended by sales or promotional materials. This work is sold with the understanding that the publisher is not engaged in rendering legal, accounting, or other professional services. Neither the publisher nor the author shall be liable for damages arising herefrom. Further, readers should be aware that Internet Websites listed in this work may have changed or disappeared between when this work was written and when it is read.

Examination Copies

Books received as examination copies in any form such as paperback and eBook are for review only and may not be made available for the use of the student. These files may not be transferred to any other party. Resale of examination copies is prohibited.

Electronic Files

The electronic file/eBook in any form of this book is licensed to the original user only and may not be transferred to any other party.

Disclaimer

The author has made sincere efforts to ensure the accuracy of the material described herein, however the author makes no warranty, expressed or implied, with respect to the quality, correctness, accuracy, or freedom from error of this document or the products it describes.

www.cadartifex.com

Dedication

First and foremost, I would like to thank my parents for being a great support throughout my career and while writing this book.

Heartfelt thanks go to all the users of **AutoCAD** textbooks published by **CADArtifex** for inspiring me in taking this challenge.

I would also like to acknowledge the efforts of the employees at CADArtifex for their dedication in editing the content of this book.

Table of Contents

Level 3: Advanced CAD Exercises .... 47 - 61

8 Table of Contents

Preface

AutoCAD, a product of Autodesk Inc., is one of the biggest technology providers to engineering, architecture, construction, manufacturing, media, and entertainment industries. It offers complete design, engineering, and entertainment solution that lets you design, visualize, simulate, and publish your ideas before they are built or created. Moreover, Autodesk continues to develop the comprehensive portfolio of state-of-art 3D software for global markets.

AutoCAD delivers a comprehensive set of productivity tools/commands that allow you to create stunning designs, speed up the documentation work, and add precision to your engineering and architectural drawings. AutoCAD is very comprehensive in its ability to create 2D and 3D drawings. With AutoCAD, you can share your designs with your clients, sub-contractors, and colleagues in smart new ways.

100 AutoCAD Exercises - Learn by Practicing (2nd Edition) book is designed to help engineers and designers interested in learning AutoCAD by practicing real-world CAD exercises. This book does not provide step-by-step instructions to create drawings in AutoCAD. Instead, it's a practice book that challenges users to first analyze the drawings and then create them using the powerful toolset of AutoCAD. This approach helps users to enhance their skills and take it to the next level. You can download all exercises used in this book for free by logging into our website (*www.cadartifex.com*).

Who Should Read This Book
This book is written with a wide range of CAD users in mind, varying from beginners to advanced users.

Prerequisites
To complete the exercises given in this book, you should have knowledge of AutoCAD. If you want to learn AutoCAD step-by-step, you can refer to *AutoCAD* textbooks published by **CADArtifex**.

What Is Covered in This Book
100 AutoCAD Exercises - Learn by Practicing (2nd Edition) book consists of 100 real-world mechanical drawings. After creating these drawings, you would be able to take your design skills to the professional level.

Download

The exercises used in this book are available for free download. To download the exercises, follow the steps given below:

1. Login to the **CADArtifex** website (*www.cadartifex.com*) by using your username and password. If you are new user, you need first to register on **CADArtifex** website as a student.

2. After login to the **CADArtifex** website, navigate to **Exercises Books > AutoCAD Exercises > 100 AutoCAD Exercises (2 Edition)**. Now, you can download the exercises of this book by using the **Exercises** drop-down list.

How to Contact the Author

We always value the feedback we receive from our readers. If you have any suggestions or feedback, please write to us at *info@cadartifex.com*. You can also provide your feedback by logging into our website *www.cadartifex.com*.

Thank you very much for purchasing *100 AutoCAD Exercises - Learn by Practicing (2nd Edition)* book, we hope that the exercises given in this book will help you to accomplish your professional goals.

100 AutoCAD Exercises
Learn by Practicing (2ⁿᵈ Edition)

Each of the 100 exercises of the book can be designed separately. No exercise is a prerequisite for another. The 100 exercises of this book are divided into three levels: 30 basic level exercises, 40 intermediate level exercises, and 30 advanced level exercises.

Level 1: 30 Basic CAD Exercises (1 to 30)

Exercise 1

Create the drawing, as shown in Figure 1.

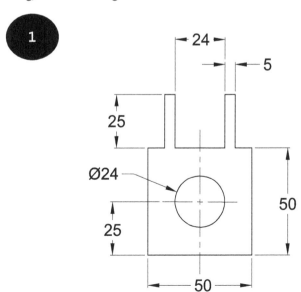

Exercise 2

Create the drawing, as shown in Figure 2.

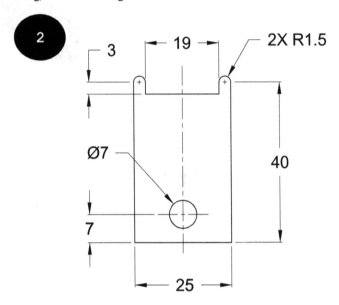

Exercise 3

Create the drawing, as shown in Figure 3.

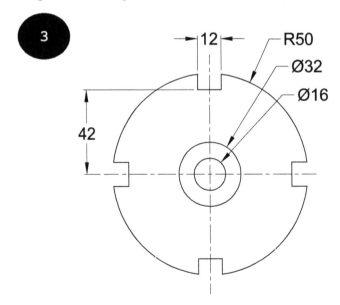

Exercise 4

Create the drawing, as shown in Figure 4.

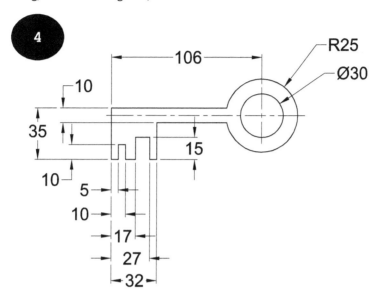

Exercise 5

Create the drawing, as shown in Figure 5.

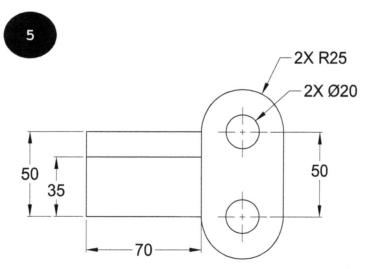

Exercise 6

Create the drawing, as shown in Figure 6.

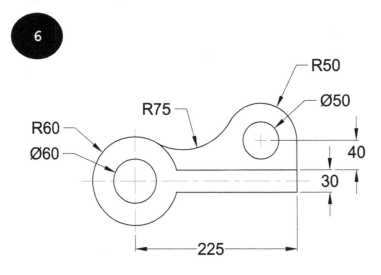

Exercise 7

Create the drawing, as shown in Figure 7.

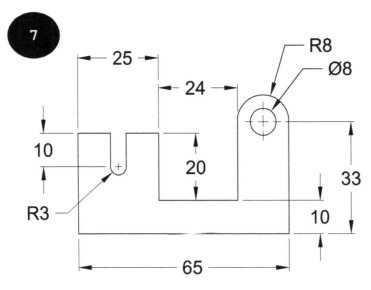

Exercise 8

Create the drawing, as shown in Figure 8.

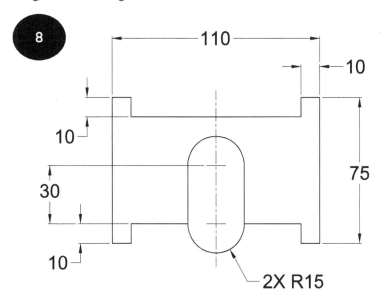

Exercise 9

Create the drawing, as shown in Figure 9.

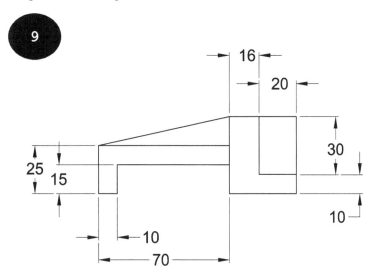

Exercise 10

Create the drawing, as shown in Figure 10.

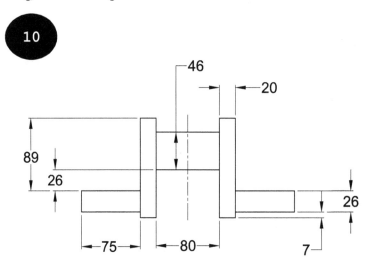

Exercise 11

Create the drawing, as shown in Figure 11.

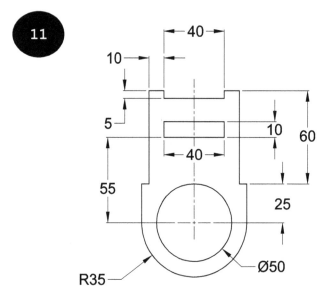

Exercise 12

Create the drawing, as shown in Figure 12.

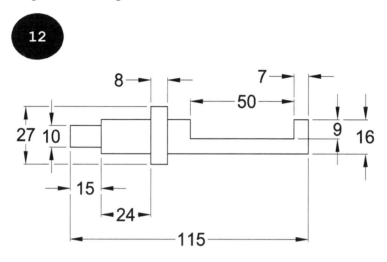

Exercise 13

Create the drawing, as shown in Figure 13.

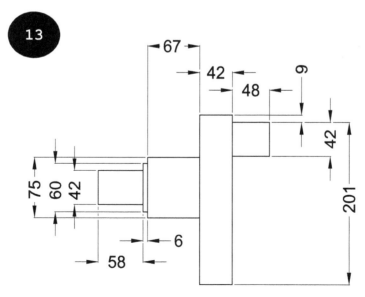

Exercise 14

Create the drawing, as shown in Figure 14.

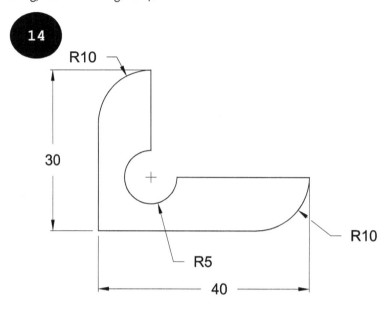

Exercise 15

Create the drawing, as shown in Figure 15.

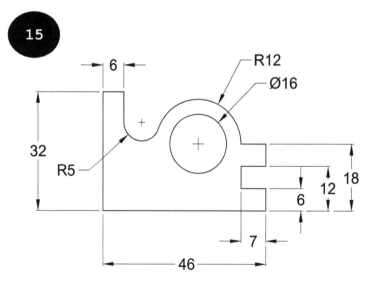

Exercise 16

Create the drawing, as shown in Figure 16.

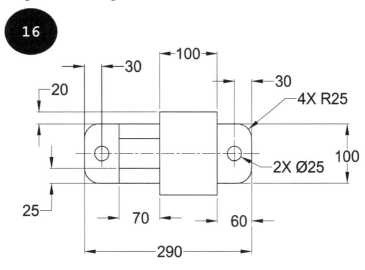

Exercise 17

Create the drawing, as shown in Figure 17.

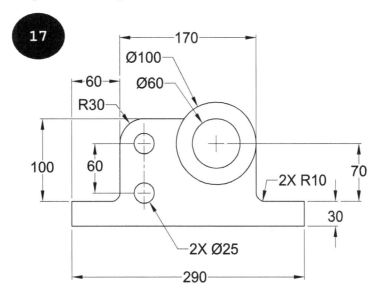

Exercise 18

Create the drawing, as shown in Figure 18.

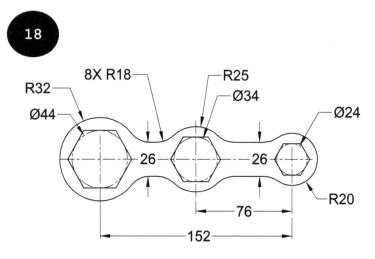

Exercise 19

Create the drawing, as shown in Figure 19.

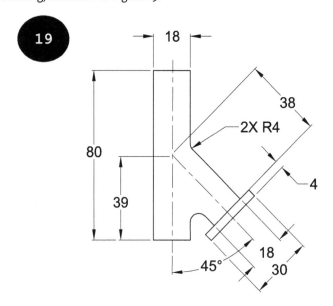

Exercise 20

Create the drawing, as shown in Figure 20.

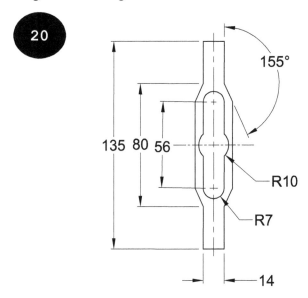

Exercise 21

Create the drawing, as shown in Figure 21.

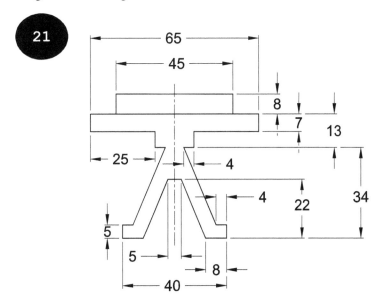

Exercise 22

Create the drawing, as shown in Figure 22.

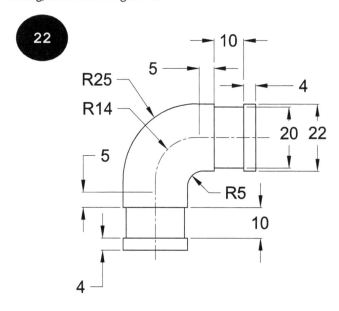

Exercise 23

Create the drawing, as shown in Figure 23.

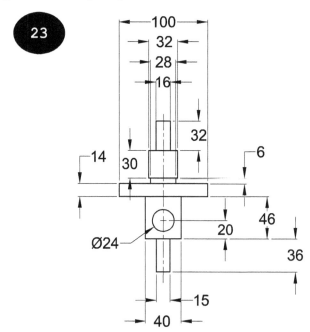

Exercise 24

Create the drawing, as shown in Figure 24.

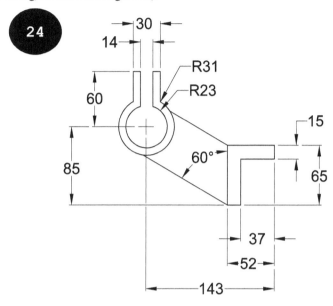

Exercise 25

Create the drawing, as shown in Figure 25.

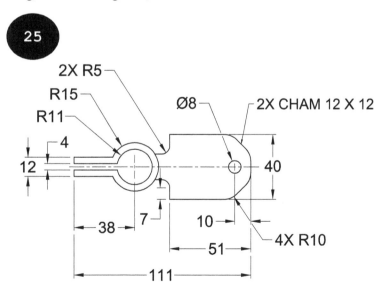

Exercise 26

Create the drawing, as shown in Figure 26.

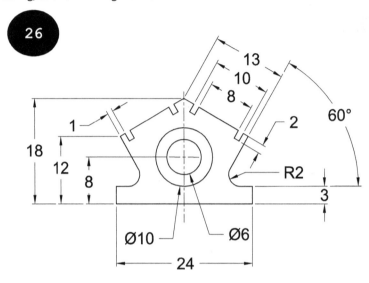

Exercise 27

Create the drawing, as shown in Figure 27.

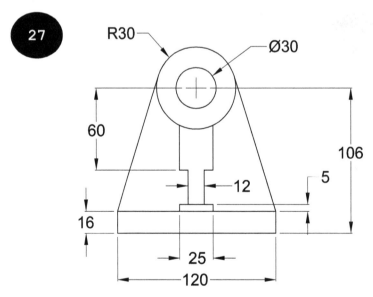

Exercise 28

Create the drawing, as shown in Figure 28.

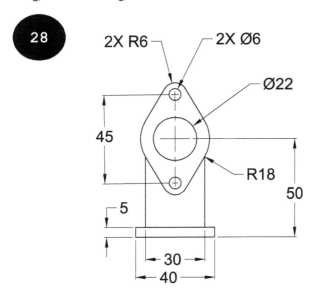

Exercise 29

Create the drawing, as shown in Figure 29.

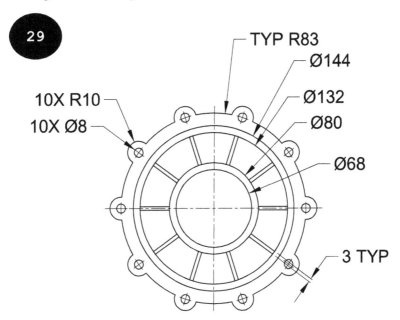

Exercise 30

Create the drawing, as shown in Figure 30.

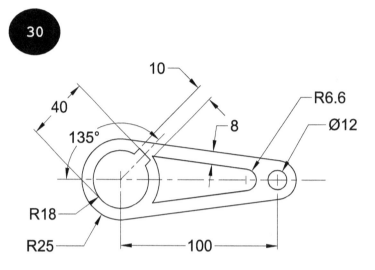

Level 2: 40 Intermediate CAD Exercises (31 to 70)

Exercise 31

Create the drawing, as shown in Figure 31.

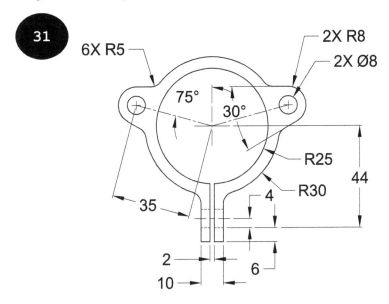

Exercise 32

Create the drawing, as shown in Figure 32.

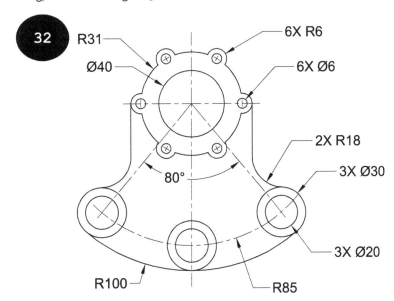

Exercise 33

Create the drawing, as shown in Figure 33.

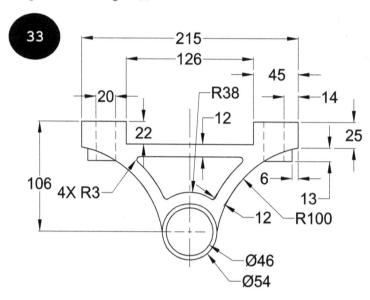

Exercise 34

Create the drawing, as shown in Figure 34.

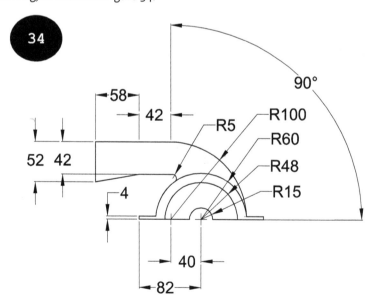

Exercise 35

Create the drawing, as shown in Figure 35.

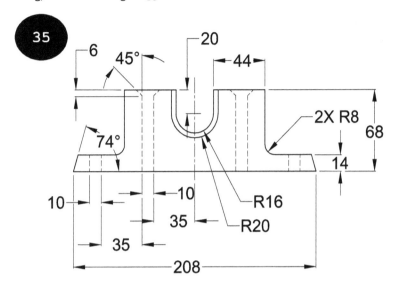

Exercise 36

Create the drawing, as shown in Figure 36.

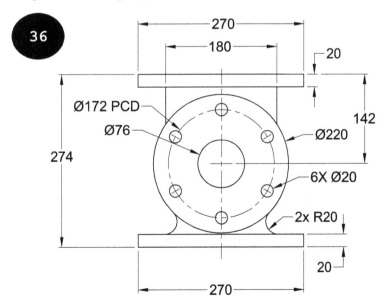

Exercise 37

Create the drawing, as shown in Figure 37.

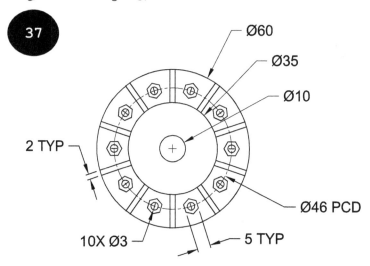

Exercise 38

Create the drawing, as shown in Figure 38.

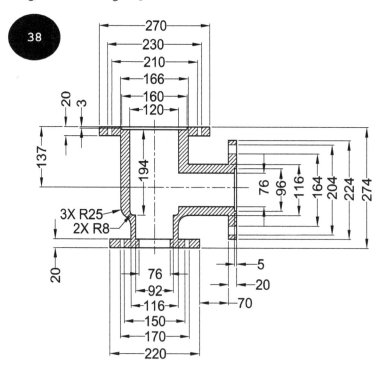

Exercise 39

Create the drawing, as shown in Figure 39.

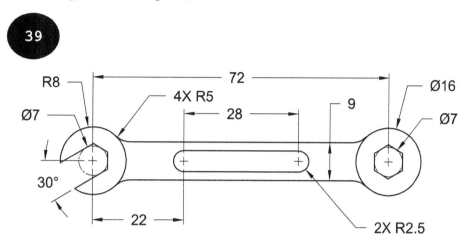

Exercise 40

Create the drawing, as shown in Figure 40.

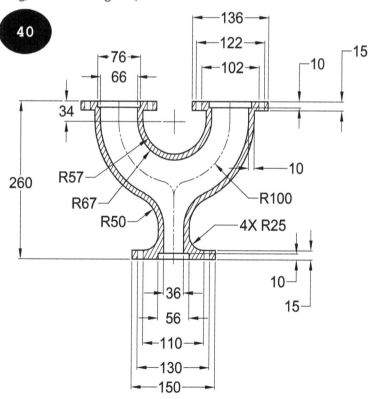

Exercise 41

Create the drawing, as shown in Figure 41.

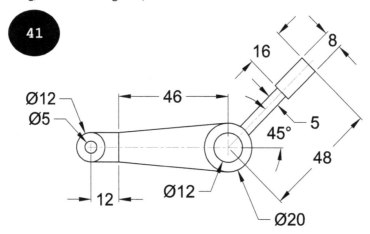

Exercise 42

Create the drawing, as shown in Figure 42.

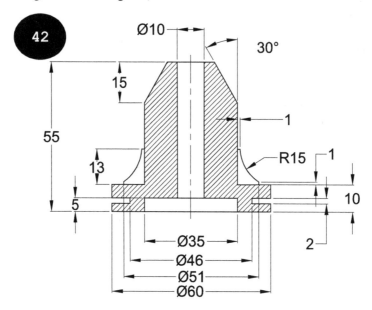

Exercise 43

Create the drawing, as shown in Figure 43.

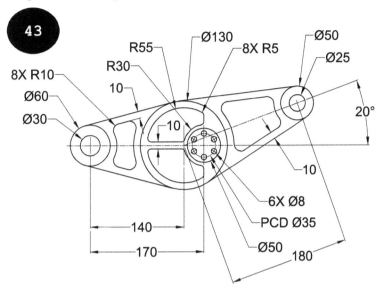

Exercise 44

Create the drawing, as shown in Figure 44.

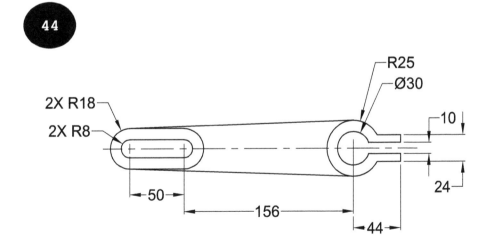

Exercise 45

Create the drawing, as shown in Figure 45.

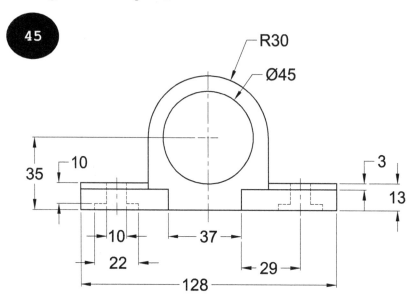

Exercise 46

Create the drawing, as shown in Figure 46.

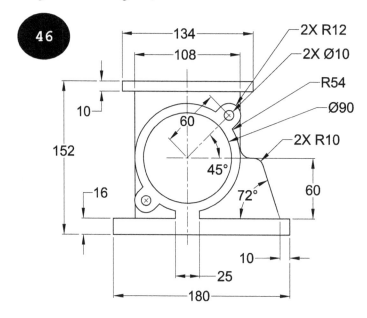

Exercise 47

Create the drawing, as shown in Figure 47.

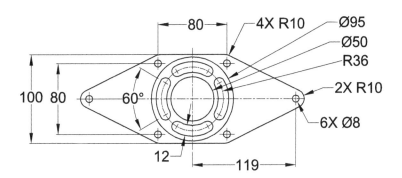

Exercise 48

Create the drawing, as shown in Figure 48.

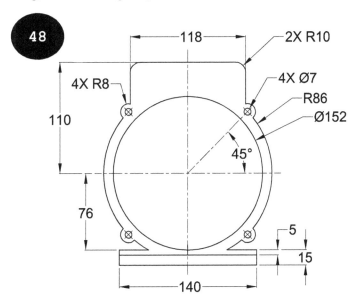

Exercise 49

Create the drawing, as shown in Figure 49.

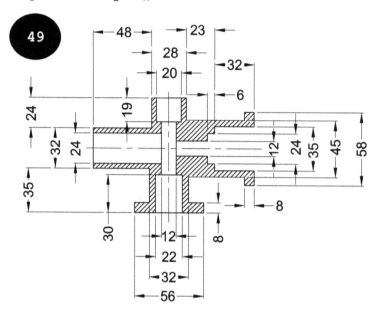

Exercise 50

Create the drawing, as shown in Figure 50.

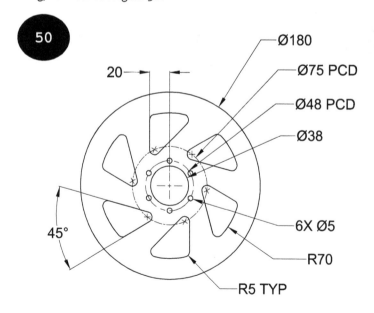

Exercise 51

Create the drawing, as shown in Figure 51.

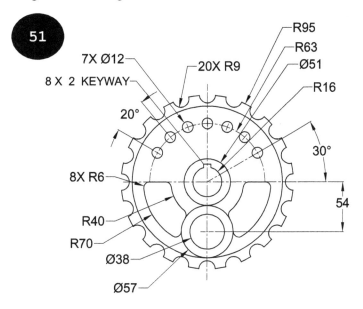

Exercise 52

Create the drawing, as shown in Figure 52.

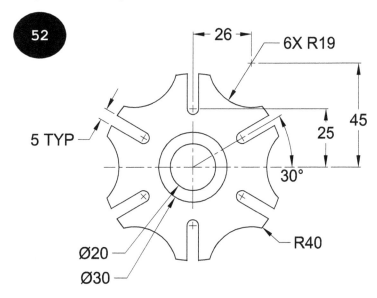

Exercise 53

Create the drawing, as shown in Figure 53.

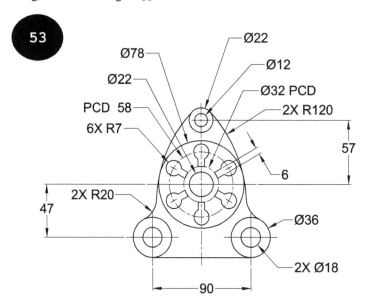

Exercise 54

Create the drawing, as shown in Figure 54.

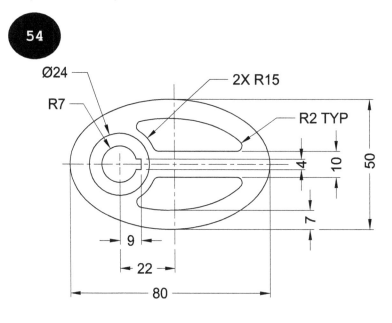

Exercise 55

Create the drawing, as shown in Figure 55.

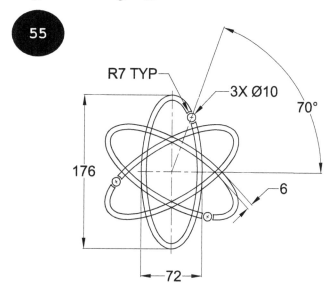

Exercise 56

Create the drawing, as shown in Figure 56.

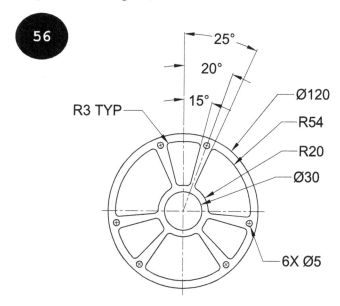

Exercise 57

Create the drawing, as shown in Figure 57.

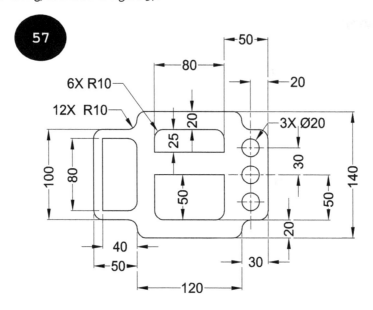

Exercise 58

Create the drawing, as shown in Figure 58.

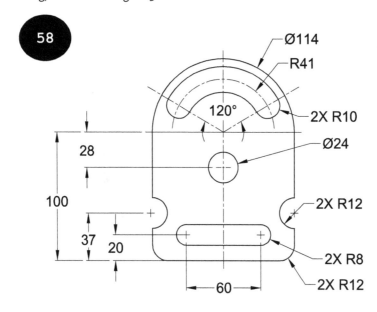

Exercise 59

Create the drawing, as shown in Figure 59.

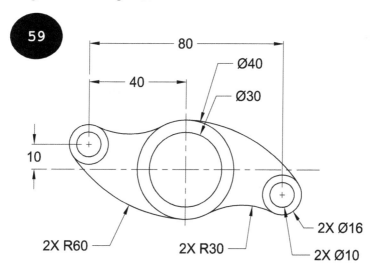

Exercise 60

Create the drawing, as shown in Figure 60.

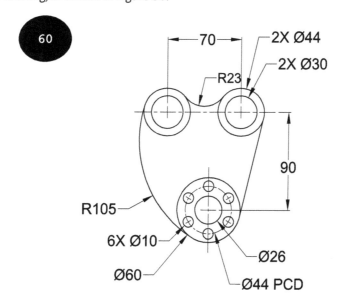

Exercise 61

Create the drawing, as shown in Figure 61.

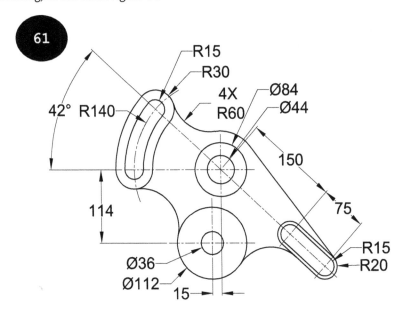

Exercise 62

Create the drawing, as shown in Figure 62.

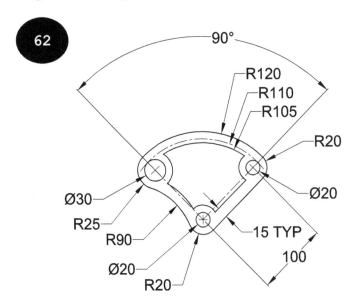

Exercise 63

Create the drawing, as shown in Figure 63.

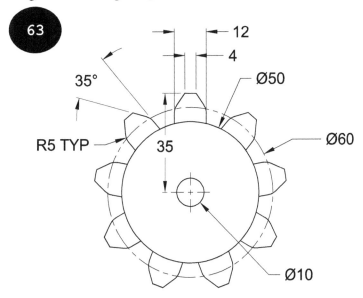

Exercise 64

Create the drawing, as shown in Figure 64.

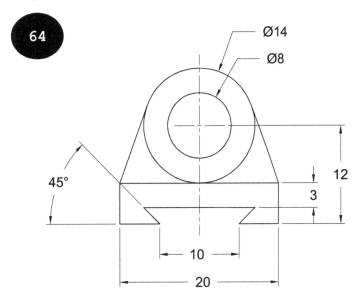

Exercise 65

Create the drawing, as shown in Figure 65.

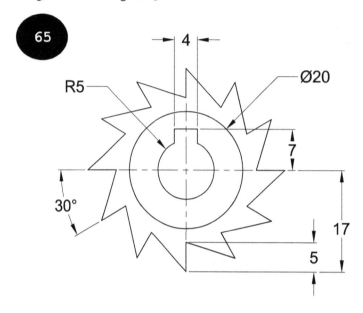

Exercise 66

Create the drawing, as shown in Figure 66.

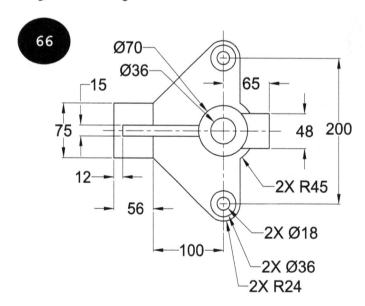

Exercise 67

Create the drawing, as shown in Figure 67.

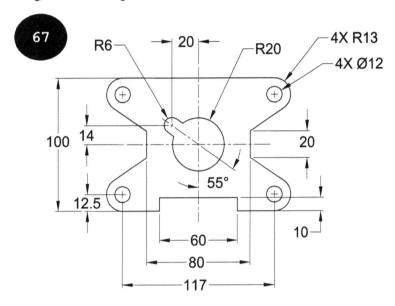

Exercise 68

Create the drawing, as shown in Figure 68.

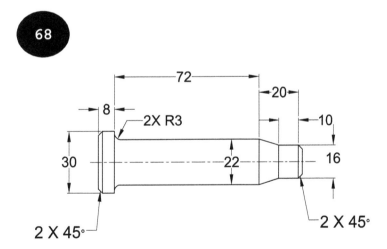

Exercise 69

Create the drawing, as shown in Figure 69.

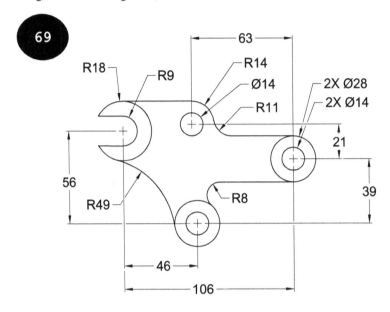

Exercise 70

Create the drawing, as shown in Figure 70.

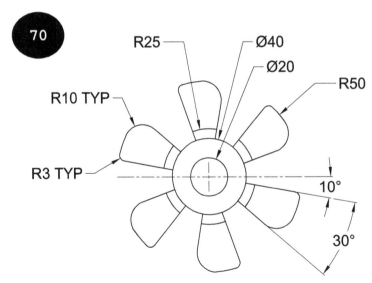

Level 3: 30 Advanced CAD Exercises (71 to 100)

Exercise 71

Create the drawing, as shown in Figure 71.

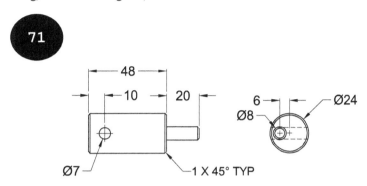

Exercise 72

Create the drawing, as shown in Figure 72.

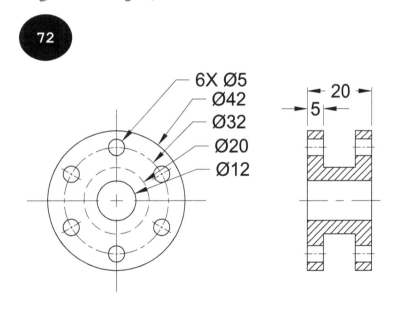

Exercise 73

Create the drawing, as shown in Figure 73.

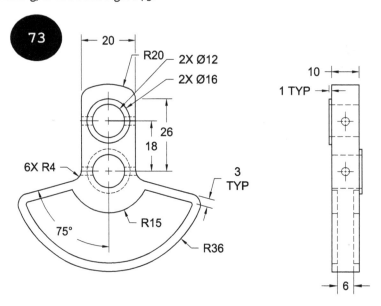

Exercise 74

Create the drawing, as shown in Figure 74.

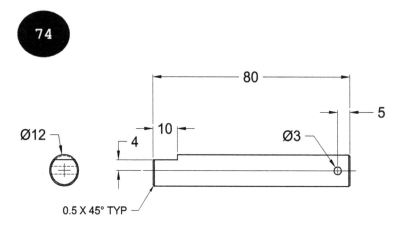

Exercise 75

Create the drawing, as shown in Figure 75.

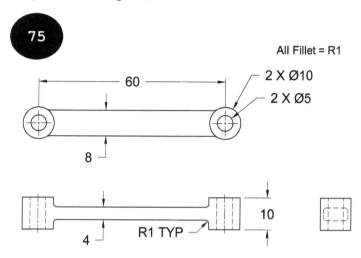

Exercise 76

Create the drawing, as shown in Figure 76.

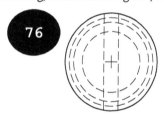

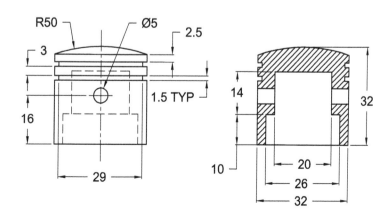

Exercise 77

Create the drawing, as shown in Figure 77.

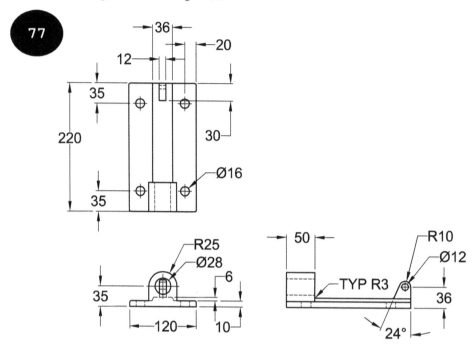

Exercise 78

Create the drawing, as shown in Figure 78.

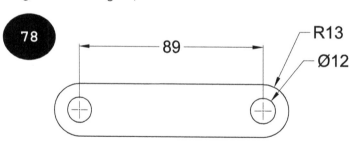

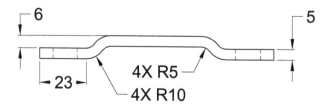

Exercise 79

Create the drawing, as shown in Figure 79.

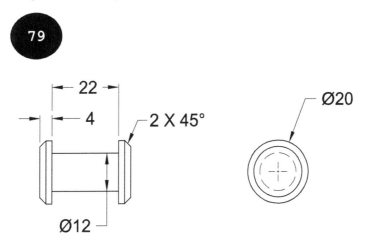

Exercise 80

Create the drawing, as shown in Figure 80.

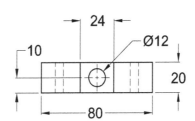
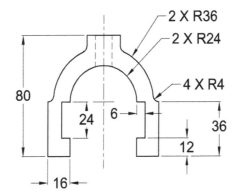

Exercise 81

Create the drawing, as shown in Figure 81.

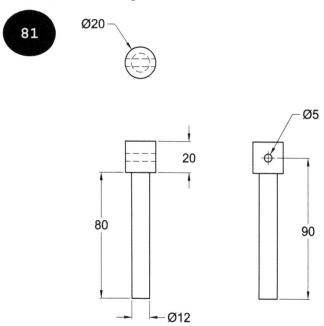

Exercise 82

Create the drawing, as shown in Figure 82.

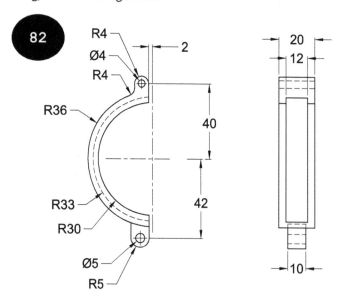

Exercise 83

Create the drawing, as shown in Figure 83.

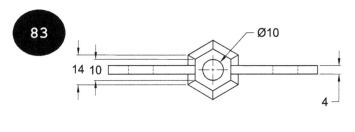

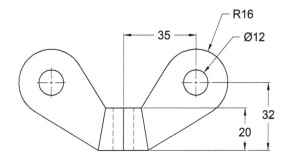

Exercise 84

Create the drawing, as shown in Figure 84.

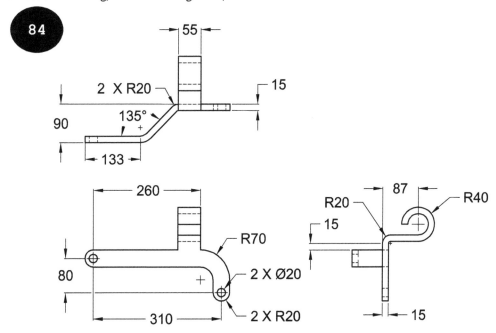

Exercise 85

Create the drawing, as shown in Figure 85.

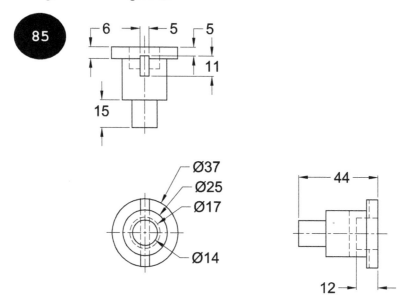

Exercise 86

Create the drawing, as shown in Figure 86.

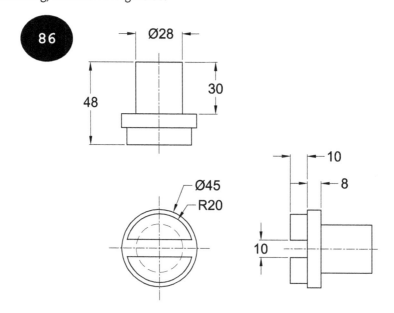

Exercise 87

Create the drawing, as shown in Figure 87.

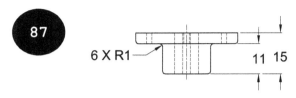

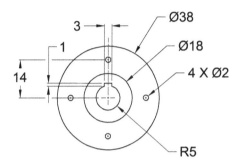

Exercise 88

Create the drawing, as shown in Figure 88.

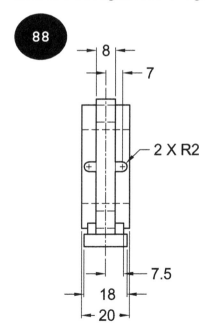

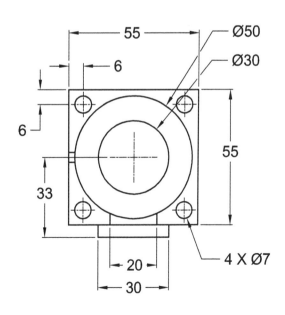

Exercise 89

Create the drawing, as shown in Figure 89.

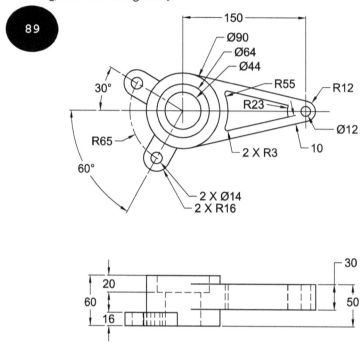

Exercise 90

Create the drawing, as shown in Figure 90.

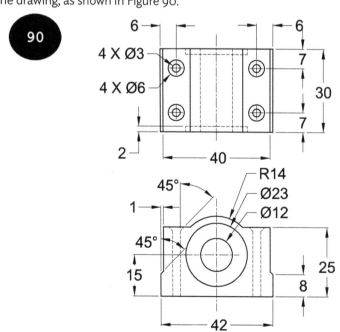

Exercise 91

Create the drawing, as shown in Figure 91.

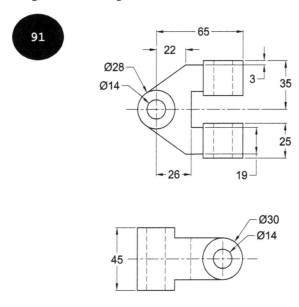

Exercise 92

Create the drawing, as shown in Figure 92.

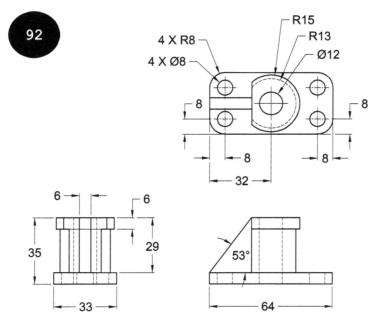

Exercise 93

Create the drawing, as shown in Figure 93.

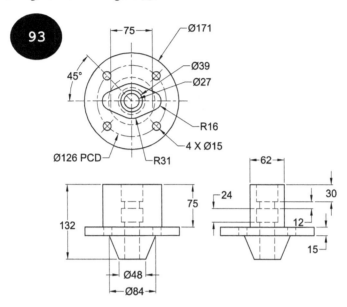

Exercise 94

Create the drawing, as shown in Figure 94.

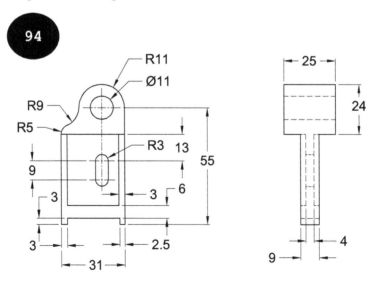

Exercise 95

Create the drawing, as shown in Figure 95.

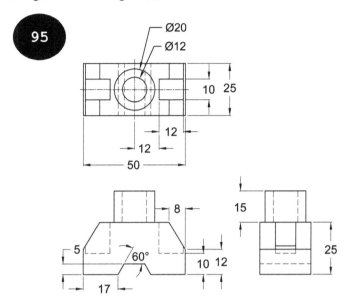

Exercise 96

Create the drawing, as shown in Figure 96.

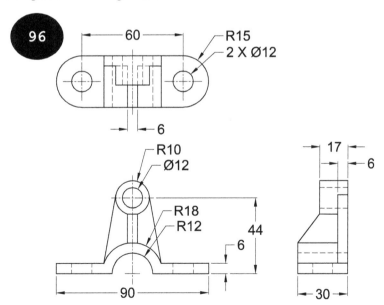

Exercise 97

Create the drawing, as shown in Figure 97.

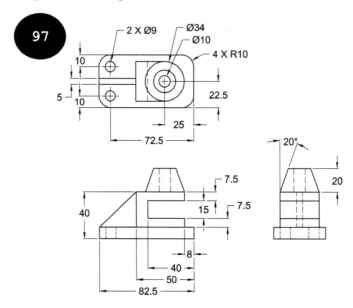

Exercise 98

Create the drawing, as shown in Figure 98.

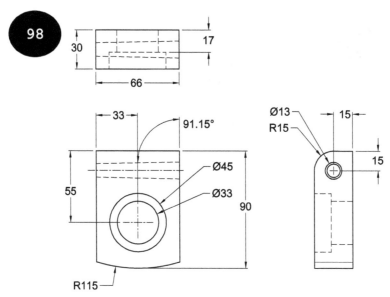

Exercise 99

Create the drawing, as shown in Figure 99.

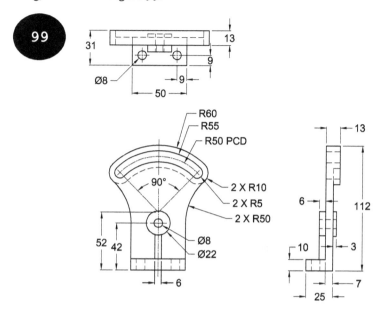

Exercise 100

Create the drawing, as shown in Figure 100.

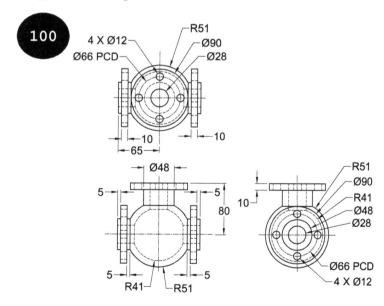

Other Publications by CADArtifex

AutoCAD Textbooks
AutoCAD 2019: A Power Guide for Beginners and Intermediate Users
AutoCAD 2018: A Power Guide for Beginners and Intermediate Users
AutoCAD 2017: A Power Guide for Beginners and Intermediate Users
AutoCAD 2016: A Power Guide for Beginners and Intermediate Users

SOLIDWORKS Textbooks
SOLIDWORKS 2019: A Power Guide for Beginners and Intermediate User
SOLIDWORKS 2018: A Power Guide for Beginners and Intermediate User
SOLIDWORKS 2017: A Power Guide for Beginners and Intermediate User
SOLIDWORKS 2016: A Power Guide for Beginners and Intermediate User
SOLIDWORKS 2015: A Power Guide for Beginners and Intermediate User

SOLIDWORKS Simulation Textbooks
SOLIDWORKS Simulation 2019: A Power Guide for Beginners and Intermediate User
SOLIDWORKS Simulation 2018: A Power Guide for Beginners and Intermediate User
Exploring Finite Element Analysis with SOLIDWORKS Simulation 2017

Autodesk Fusion 360 Textbooks
Autodesk Fusion 360: A Power Guide for Beginners and Intermediate User (2 Edition)
Autodesk Fusion 360: A Power Guide for Beginners and Intermediate User (1 Edition)

Creo Parametric Textbooks
Creo Parametric 5.0: A Power Guide for Beginners and Intermediate User
Creo Parametric 4.0: A Power Guide for Beginners and Intermediate User

Exercises Books
SOLIDWORKS Exercises - Learn by Practicing

www.ingramcontent.com/pod-product-compliance
Lightning Source LLC
Chambersburg PA
CBHW082112070326
40689CB00052B/4616